{journey through john}
a lenten devotional book

Drew Filkins

THE
PEOPLES
CHURCH

Journey through John: a Lenten Devotional Book.

Design by Andrew Filkins

ISBN-13: 978-1495936043
ISBN-10: 149593604X

Holly, thank you for your love and support.

Journey through John
Lent 2014

Table of Contents

{preface}

Lent is a sacred time of prayer, penance, sacrifice and good works in preparation for the celebration of the resurrection of Jesus Christ. Followers of Christ have used this time to fast, focus on scripture and engage in spiritual disciplines. In the past The Peoples Church has used this season to focus on a single book within scripture. This year we are going to journey through the fourth gospel, John.

In the Liturgical calendar, Lent is the season between Ash Wednesday and Easter. It starts with remembering the frailty and brevity of life on Ash Wednesday. Throughout the following six weeks, we lament the broken nature of humanity and the world. While this season can appear to dwell on the melancholy, it is meant to be a time of reflection. We hold one hand in the present age of despair but groan and long for the coming redemption God has promised to both us and creation.

Lent ends with Holy Week. It is during this time that we remember Christ gathering his disciples and sharing a meal with them, being betrayed by a friend and ultimately receiving a death sentence. While this all may seem a bit dark, it is the capstone of the Christian faith, reminding us that while the world, humanity and even our lives seem to be headed toward destruction, resurrection is actually on its way.

I hope this book will give us a time to reflect on the identity of Christ and will help us to ask the question: who is this Jesus? John has shown through his gospel what Christ has done and is doing in the world, as well as how we might meet Christ in his actions to redeem and renew this broken creation. I am looking forward to hearing how God is using our journey to help us connect, grow, serve and share like Christ has demonstrated.

Pastor Drew

{introduction}

How do we become acquainted with a stranger?

How does that stranger become a friend?

And how does that friend become a member of your family?

The story of Jesus Christ has been told and retold to believers who walked side by side with him before his resurrection as well as by people like you and me who have encountered this same Christ in all manners of people and places in our lives. Yet how do our personal stories, interactions, and private narratives ever come close to providing the full and true identity of Jesus from Nazareth, who was called the Messiah, the Son of God, the true light in the darkness?

The four gospels we encounter in the New Testament, Matthew, Mark, Luke and John, each take a unique approach to addressing this question of identity as they seek to share the good news of Jesus' life, death, resurrection, and ascension with the world so that all might believe. The gospels are as varied as the people who have come to follow Jesus these past two thousand years and we should never limit our view of Christ to one story, one moment, or one account. We see, hear, and interact with Jesus together and alone, through the gospels and through our community.

There is something extremely powerful about sharing a story together. When reading a book aloud with my children, there are shared words that spark our individual imaginations to picture, envision, and dream what is or has occurred. The same holds true when we read the words from scripture

6

together as a community. This year, the congregation at The Peoples Church of East Lansing is reading the fourth gospel together as a community. Each day includes a passage from John's good news account of Jesus and with each passage, we have thoughts to ponder and questions to consider. We will continue this journey through John as we wrestle with the identity of Jesus yesterday, today and tomorrow.

We are indebted to our associate pastor, Drew Filkins, for his tireless work on this project. Each day, Pastor Drew offers initial thoughts to prepare us for the daily reading before listing the passage scheduled for the day. After reading the selection, he leaves us with questions to discern and pray over during our day. Let this study be an opportunity for you to become reacquainted of the Christ who came for all people in order to reconcile them back to God, to one another, to ourselves, and to creation. Thank you for joining with us in this journey and may God bless your interactions with the living Lord who continues to lead us to the promised kingdom of peace.

Andrew Pomerville
Senior Pastor, The Peoples Church East Lansing

Journey through John
Lent 2014

Ash Wednesday, March 5
Imposition of Ashes
12 p.m. & 6:30 p.m. Sanctuary

The clouds covering the sky deepened the darkness of the rural area I was traveling. I could only see where my headlights shown. However, I was surprised at how well I could see other cars' headlights as they approached in the dark. Their light pierced the darkness and drove it away.

John begins his gospel by retelling the creation poem from Genesis 1-2, where the Word, Jesus, is central to this creative process. In the beginning was the Word. This idea of creation and new creation are central to the fourth gospel. He frames the gospel account with the creation poem language and symbolism. He wants us to see that Jesus is not just a historical figure but the totality of history itself.

This Word, Jesus, came into the world because the world had become a dark place. We can see this darkness around us through wars, famines, and natural disasters; in our friends and family through illness, depression and addiction; and in our own lives through broken relationships, loneliness and heartbreak. It is on Ash Wednesday that we recognize the frailty of life, our mortality, and the brokenness of the world. We remember that we were formed from dust, and to dust we will return. It is a solemn moment in the church calendar.

But like a story we have read many times before, we know the ending. We know that although it looks like darkness and death have the final word, John will show us again that the light and resurrection have the final word. Although it seems that a thick darkness has had the final say, light has come into the world and his name is Jesus.

{think}

What do you think these verses say about Jesus' identity?

{reflect}

Where do you see darkness in the world, in our community and in your own life?

{act}

How can we join Jesus in being the light in dark places?

{pray}

Ask God to reveal where you can be light in dark places and what actions you can take to help bring his light.

Journey through John
Lent 2014

Thursday, March 6

Signposts are not a destination, but rather a way of pointing us toward where we want to go. When I am driving north to cross the Mackinaw Bridge, I don't look at the sign for the bridge as the destination. It would seem silly to stop and take my picture next to the sign for the bridge instead of continuing on to the beautiful, magnificent structure itself.

As you read this gospel, look for the ways that John the Baptist is pointing people to Jesus and his coming kingdom. John the Baptist appears in all four Gospel accounts. Each writer seems to view him as an important necessary part of the story. John is an odd man saying peculiar things in the wilderness.

In today's passage, you will find a great story where John is preaching, gaining followers and baptizing with little ego of his own involved. After John makes these grand statements about Jesus, he baptizes him. The next day as John is teaching two of his disciples Jesus happens by and John declares again, "Behold the Lamb of God!" These two disciples, one of named Andrew, leave to follow Jesus. John does not seem disturbed that his disciples abandon him to follow this Rabbi, Jesus.

Andrew then seeks out his brother, Peter, to tell him that he has found this Lamb of God and points Peter toward Jesus.

{think}

In what ways does John point others to Jesus?

{reflect}

Why would each John, the Gospel writer, and John, the Baptist, refer to Jesus as the Lamb of God?

{act}

How can we declare with the same enthusiasm that Jesus is the Lamb of God?

{pray}

Ask God to use you to point people toward Jesus as the Lamb of God through your actions and words.

**Journey through John
Lent 2014**

Friday, March 7

Jesus' first miracle is turning water into wine? This doesn't quite seem right. Jesus is supposed to make the blind see the wonderful world around them, the deaf hear beautiful songs and to make the lame jump with joy. But, water into wine? Not exactly what we might expect!

Weddings in first century Palestine were weeklong affairs. The family would host their guests as they celebrated this new union. The family was expected to supply the food and wine for the duration of the celebration. It would be an embarrassment to come up short.

The Hebrew Prophets declared time and time again that one of the traits of the coming Messiah was an abundance of the good things in life, including food and wine. In fact, wine would flow from the mountains. An abundance of wine would point toward the Messianic age, when God would break into creation to set his people free.

The author begins numbering the signs Jesus performs and we are expected to continue counting. These seven signs point us toward the ultimate sign of God's love for creation and humanity, Christ's resurrection. It is through this that new life and new creation are made possible.

As you read the Gospel of John record the miracles or signs John reports in Appendix A (page 108).

Read John 2v1-25, focusing on v1-12

{think}

What does Jesus' interaction with his mother tells us about his character?

{reflect}

Why would Jesus hide this miracle from the party host and guests but allow his disciples, the servants, and his mother know?

{act}

How can you show God's abundant love and grace to your family, the community and the world?

{pray}

Pray that we might witness the signs of God's love in our families, our community and the world.

Journey through John
Lent 2014

In seventh grade, I attended my first Shakespearean play. I was excited and I can remember what my drama teacher told me about watching the play. He said, "You are not going to catch every phrase and idea. Some of it is going to be confusing. Just let the words wash over you. The more you hear, read, or watch Shakespeare, the more you will get it." This is how I feel about the discourses in John.

Jesus uses language, metaphors and ideas that are not familiar to us. We have to be born of what? When we are born of the Spirit, we will begin acting like the wind? Jesus has to be lifted up like Moses lifted a snake? Then John goes right into one of most well known verses in the Bible, John 3v16.

Jesus and Nicodemus knew that being born into the right family was highly important for an individual's advancement in society. But Jesus seems to be saying that in the coming kingdom there are different standards for advancement. Our earthly heritage will not matter but our spiritual heritage will. With this in mind, we head into the most famous verse of the gospel, as well as those following.

Read John 3v1-21, focusing on v16-21

{think}

What do you find interesting about the verses that follow John 3v16?

{reflect}

Why did Jesus come in to the world?

{act}

How can we make sure that we will not be part of the condemned?

{pray}

Pray that The Peoples Church (or your home congregation) might be a community living out the truth before a watching world.

Journey through John
Lent 2014

{lectionary passages}

Old Testament Reading
Psalm 32

New Testament Reading
Matthew 4v1-11

{sermon notes}

{think}

What spoke to you during the worship service today?

{reflect}

What was the call on your heart today?

{act}

What is something you are going to do or do differently because you encountered God today?

{pray}

Praises   Concerns

**Journey through John
Lent 2014**

Monday, March 10

It is a very human emotion to be jealous. I witnessed it in my children from a very early age. One of them will have a toy and the other one will want it without having thought of it mere seconds before. Or one will be getting my wife's attention and the other will come in and make such a commotion to draw her attention and claim that important place.

Jealousy is a very dangerous thing. This could have consumed John. He had been preaching and baptizing in the wilderness and gaining quite a following. Now this newcomer, Jesus, shows up and he begins to preach and baptize. To add insult to injury, people begin to leave John to become a disciple of Jesus. But somehow John finds a way not to be jealous of what Jesus is doing but rather he continues to point people toward Jesus.

As you read today's passage, think about how John could have been defeated by watching his disciples leave to follow Jesus, but instead finds his place in the history of God's people.

{think}

In what ways does John deflect the concerns that people are leaving him to follow Jesus?

{reflect}

Why do we become jealous of other churches, ministries and/or Christians?

{act}

How can we move people from following one another to truly following Jesus as John did?

{pray}

Pray that when people see you and our church community we are signposts pointing towards Christ and not ourselves.

**Journey through John
Lent 2014**

Tuesday, March 11

Growing up, my family owned ten acres of hunting property just south of Kalkaska, MI. It was great place. It had a little camping trailer that no longer moved, but we had heat and a place go when it rained. With no running water, we had to carry five gallon containers to the neighbor's house, which was just down the road, fill them and bring them back. We did this a few times a day when our family would visit during the summer. I now better appreciate having hot and cold water flow instantly from any faucet at my house.

In first century Palestine, most cities or communities would have a common well from which the women would come and draw water for their household needs. Most women would go during the morning or evening, the cool parts of the day, to get their water. It had a tendency to become a daily social event. It is here we find Jesus sitting by this well in the middle of the afternoon, having a conversation with a woman he should not only avoid, but shun and condemn.

The Samaritans were hated by the Jews. They were Jews who had intermarried with the Gentiles and had polluted the pure bloodline of God's chosen people. Therefore, the Jews despised them; yet it is with a Samaritan woman of ill-repute that Jesus had this unconventional interaction.

Read John 4v1-42, focusing on v1-26

{think}

In what ways does the woman misunderstand Jesus and what he is saying?

{reflect}

Why might the woman change the conversation when Jesus tells her about her personal life (v. 19-20)?

{act}

How might interacting with Jesus require us to modify our behavior?

{pray}

It is through Christ's powerful interaction with this woman that she brings her whole town out to see Jesus. Pray that we all have powerful encounters with Jesus that drive us to share his message of grace and love with all of our community.

**Journey through John
Lent 2014**

Wednesday, March 12

A friend of mine went to Ireland to work and minister for six months. He loved the people, the culture and the beautiful scenery. When he came back to the States, people would ask him about his experience and then they would say over and over again to him, "I really want to go to Ireland one day." To this he would reply, "Do you really want to go? Have you looked into it? Have you set a date? Have you checked on airfare? Do you really want to go or do you just want to say you want to go?" While he could have replied with a little more charm, there is a powerful point behind his statement.

In today's passage we discover Jesus healing two different people. The first is a royal official whose son is ill. He comes to Jesus, begging him to heal his son and Jesus heals him from a distance of about 20 miles. The son is healed the very moment Jesus tells the father, "Your son will live." John reminds us to keep counting the signs or miracles by telling us this is the second sign Jesus performed. It is also the last time he helps us with the numbering process. However, he immediately enters into another story of Jesus healing a lame man.

Jesus goes to a shrine where lame people would lie in hope of being the first one in the water when bubbles would appear. It was believed that the first person in would be healed. There was a man who had been lame for 38 years lying next to the pool. We are to assume that he has been there for a while, probably years. Jesus asks him a very odd question, "Do you want to get better?" and I would add, "or do you just want to say you want to get better?"

Continue to record signs in Appendix A (page 108).

Read John 4v43-5v15 focusing on 5v1-9

{think}

What strikes you as odd in the discourse between Jesus and the lame man?

{reflect}

In what areas of your life have you allowed sickness, problems or sin to become your identity?

{act}

How can we each "pick up mats and walk" in areas in our own lives that have become lame?

{pray}

Pray that Jesus' healing power might manifest itself in your life in areas of sin, illness or problems.

Journey through John
Lent 2014

Thursday, March 13

Some of my fondest memories as a child involve fishing with my dad. We would usually head off to the river on weekdays allowing me to skip school. He showed me how to spot the fish, where they liked to hide, what flies to use to catch them, how to cast, how to fight the fish and, most importantly, how to land the fish to get the picture of it. It was my fishing apprenticeship. I learned at his side to do the same things he did and to love fly fishing.

Jesus has been questioned about his breaking of the Sabbath law. He had healed the lame man on the Sabbath. The Jewish leaders were not happy that Jesus was teaching ideas that were usurping their power and they decided that they needed to do something about this Jesus.

What might have made the Jewish leaders even more upset than the breaking of the Sabbath law was Jesus calling God his father. They realized that if God was Jesus' Father, then he was saying he is like his Father, divine. Jesus doesn't run away from this idea. Rather, embraces it. He tells those who are listening to him that he is not only the son of God but also the apprentice of God, learning the trade of love, grace and resurrection.

Read John 5v16-47 focusing on 5v19-29

{think}

What are parts of the "trade" that Jesus is learning from God?

{reflect}

Why is it important that Jesus is about the business of the Father?

{act}

Where can the followers of Jesus be at work like the Father and Son are at work?

{pray}

Ask Jesus to show you where he is at work and to grant you the courage to join him.

Journey through John
Lent 2014

Friday, March 14

When I was about 11 years old, a friend of our family took us out on Lake Huron in his 18 foot ski boat. We had a wonderful day exploring an island, having a picnic lunch and swimming. Late in the afternoon, we noticed the wind beginning to pick up and larger waves beginning to form. So we headed for the dock. As we traversed the water, the swells approached to six feet. The boat would ride up one side of the wave and then slam into the other side. I was never so happy to see a dock in my entire life. The water can be beautiful and refreshing but also treacherous.

Jesus had just fed the five thousand and they were ready to make him king by force. Knowing that this was not God's plan for his coronation, he withdrew to the mountain by himself. His disciples left to cross the lake without Jesus. During the crossing the wind grew strong and the waves became daunting.

We must remember that for the ancient world, as for many today, water is dangerous and daunting. While travel across land was dangerous enough, sailing was much more so. Without the Coast Guard, GPS or many of the safety devices that we have today, the sea was a place of fear, danger and loss. For Jesus to walk on the sea is more than just a show of power but an overcoming of the unknown, danger, loss and fear.

This story of Jesus walking on water is a demonstration that he is Lord over all the dangerous, unknown and treacherous parts of our lives.

Read John 6v1-24, focusing on v16-24

{think}

How is this account different from the other accounts of Jesus walking on the water? (Mark 6:45-52)

{reflect}

Identify times in your life or in the life of someone close to you that have felt like the disciples rowing in a storm.

{act}

How can you be the presence of Jesus to someone who is rowing through the storms of life?

{pray}

Pray for those you know personally, indirectly and around the world who might be going through various storms in their lives.

**Journey through John
Lent 2014**

Growing up, my mother baked our bread. It was a wonderful French bread with a crispy crust and a fluffy center. My father, brother and I would wait with bated breath for it to come out of the oven. We loved the smell of the bread baking, the look of the golden brown crust and the steam that poured out as we cut into the loaf. We would eat most of a piping hot loaf with butter, fighting over who got the heels. Bread holds a special place in my memories.

In the passage today, Jesus tells his listeners, "I am the bread of life." He has just turned a few loaves of bread into enough to feed thousands and now that crowd is following him. Jesus takes what is a staple in their lives, bread, and turns it into a metaphor about himself. Not only are some hungry every-day for physical bread to fill their stomachs but there are also those hunger for the one who can sustain them today and into eternity.

The new way of being human that Jesus is showing the world is for what humanity has hungered. They have longed to be filled with an abundant, eternal life that does not just start some "one day" but today. This bread, Jesus, makes abundant eternal life possible today and forever.

Jesus makes seven "I Am" statements in the gospel of John. As you read through the gospel, record the "I am" statements in Appendix B (page 109).

Read John 6v25-59, focusing on v25-40

{think}

In what ways does Jesus liken himself to bread? How does Jesus say he is better than bread?

{reflect}

Why would Jesus seem to chastise the people who followed him around the lake (v25-27)?

{act}

How can we make sure people have their daily bread and know Christ as the true source of daily sustenance?

{pray}

Pray for people in our community that need bread today, both physical and spiritual.

Journey through John
Lent 2014

Sunday, March 16

{lectionary passages}

Old Testament Reading
Genesis 12:1-4

New Testament Reading
Romans 4:1-5, 13-17

{sermon notes}

{think}

What spoke to you during the worship service today?

{reflect}

What was the call on your heart today?

{act}

What is something you are going to do or do differently because you encountered God today?

{pray}

Praises   Concerns

**Journey through John
Lent 2014**

Monday, March 17

I find it hard to sit and listen to lectures when a speaker challenges my worldview. However, I will sit for hours to hear a theologian with whom I agree pontificate about grand ideas. When a theologian tries to convince me of a view I think errant, I easily get annoyed, even angry, and I will possibly leave. I wish this was not true, but all too often it is.

We found Jesus giving hard lessons in our reading last Saturday, and now some of his followers are leaving. Jesus disrupted their worldview. Similarly, today, many people want following Christ to be just spiritual or just physical. Jesus does not see the world in this way. In this passage, as Jesus speaks about himself ascending and staying on earth He is saying that he is as comfortable on earth as in heaven. Jesus is not just concerned with our spiritual life but our physical being as well. He does not want people to follow him for the free bread but because he is their sustenance. Humanity was made to be both physical and spiritual.

All the gospel writers have a moment when they define those who are the Twelve - this is John's account. He does not record their names but rather that they remain with him. All the other followers, disciples, were grumbling and deserting Jesus. The Twelve who remained were Jesus' chosen ones, even the one who is going to betray him.

{think}

In what ways do you find Jesus' teaching hard?

{reflect}

Why would Jesus give such difficult teachings if he knew people would desert him?

{act}

How can we balance the messages of compassion with the more difficult messages of Jesus?

{pray}

Pray that you might remain with Jesus even when you discover difficult teachings that test your worldview.

**Journey through John
Lent 2014**

Tuesday, March 18

I am a stickler for rules when it comes to games. These are not only the rules that actually govern the game but also the rules that my family has made up to make the game more fun. My wife and I were playing a bid euchre game with friends one night. All the people had played this game or one similar in different contexts and knew the general rules. However, I made sure that we played by a rule that I am sure only members in my family play by. I wanted to know that everyone was keeping my rules for the game correctly.

Jesus' popularity and infamy were both growing. People were coming to see Jesus either because they loved to listen to him or because they thought he was of the devil. There were people who wanted to kill Jesus. This is why Jesus secretly went to the Festival of Tabernacles. Jesus declared that what he was teaching was not of his own accord but rather from the Father. This would have made some people even angrier with Jesus. They had their rules about how the laws were to be lived and Jesus was changing all the rules, saying his version was from God.

The religious leaders were normally the ones who trained and gave authority to those who wanted to teach. However, Jesus was teaching with great authority that had not been authorized or taught by the religious leaders but from another source. This scared them, not only because of the loss of control, but because their rules were being challenged; much like I get upset when someone challenged one of my rules during a card game, though the stakes in this case were much greater.

{think}

In what ways has Jesus challenged the religious leaders and their rules so far in the Gospel of John?

{reflect}

Why do we hold so tightly to our ways of understanding the laws and rules that God has given us?

{act}

How can we better discern (judge)?

{pray}

Pray that we might allow God to show us that compassion, mercy and forgiveness are far better than judgment.

**Journey through John
Lent 2014**

When it comes to a powerful, dynamic leader, people are often torn between thinking the person is crazy or genius. Steve Jobs, at Apple Corp., was such a person. While his methods of leadership and inspiration were not mainstream, the innovations he brought to personal computing have been astounding. Those who worked with him seemed to love him or hate him; though very few seemed to be in the middle.

Jesus was also a powerful, dynamic leader, very much different than Steve Jobs. Jesus cared for and identified with the common people, the poor and the outcast. If you wanted to be a great leader in that day, as today, you'd needed to buddy up with those who were already in power. Jesus did not. He declared a kingdom where the first will be last and the last, first.

The common people seemed to love Jesus while the first century Jewish leaders wanted him dead because he was, in their eyes, blaspheming. This transgression of the Torah was punishable by stoning. But the Jewish leaders were not ready to bring him in yet because of Jesus' popularity with the people, including the temple guards. The people were divided on who they thought Jesus was. Some thought he was a prophet, still other the Messiah, and the Jewish leaders thought he was a lunatic. These ideas about who Jesus is still confront us today.

{think}

What reasons does each group have for thinking of Jesus in differently?

{reflect}

Why do people view Jesus uniquely and what can we learn from these varying perspectives?

{act}

How can we declare who the true Jesus is through our words and deeds?

{pray}

Pray that we believe and act more like Jesus; so that a stream of living water will pour out of us onto a thirsty world.

Journey through John
Lent 2014

Thursday, March 20

During my graduate studies there was an older gentleman who was in many of my classes. We became friends and often enjoyed lunches together. One of the things that I admired about him was that when I would ask him a question about a theological idea or biblical passage and would expect usually one of the two most common views or ideas, he would surprise me with another way to think about it. What a wonderful skill - not to be polarizing but to find a third way to think, work and live in the world.

Today's reading continues Jesus' interactions with the Pharisees and teachers of the law. They are continually trying to trap him. While this story is not found in the earliest manuscripts of John, it is a wonderful story nevertheless. A woman caught in adultery is brought before Jesus by the teachers of the law. They quote the law to Jesus and ask him what they should do with her. They want him either to condemn her to death and lose the favor of the people or to have mercy on her and show that he does not follow the law. Jesus finds a third way: a better way.

{think}

How does Jesus surprise you in this passage?

{reflect}

What do you think Jesus was writing in the sand and why?

{act}

How can we break out of polarizing patterns of speech and activities to find a better way, a more Christ-like way?

{pray}

Pray that we might be a church that does not fall into the polarizing speech and actions of the world but leads in finding the third way.

**Journey through John
Lent 2014**

Most often when we hear about a crime on the local evening news, it is followed by "If you have any information about this event, call…" Eyewitnesses tell a jury what happened but often one witness is not enough to convict a criminal. There needs to be more. In the Torah, testimonies had to be verified by two witnesses.

The Israelites were supposed to bring light to the world but too often they had been providing darkness. God had blessed Israel so that they could be a blessing to the other nations. Instead, they horded the blessing for themselves.

Now Jesus came claiming to be the light of the world. He was going to accomplish what Israel could not. The blessing he received he now poured out on the widow, the orphan, the poor, and the outcast. He included those who had been excluded. The teachers of the law were asking, "Where does he get his authority to do this?" They were putting him on trial and asking for witnesses.

Read John 8v12-30, focusing on v12-20

{think}

In what ways do we reject the light that has come into the world?

{reflect}

Why do you think Jesus' argument about his witness being valid is appropriate and why might it not hold up in court?

{act}

How can we testify to who Jesus is in all our encounters with those outside the church?

{pray}

Pray that God might reveal the places where darkness is still present in your life, our church and our world and ask Jesus to bring his light into those areas.

Saturday, March 22

One of the things I love the most is a powerful conclusion to a sermon. It does not need to answer all the questions but it is wonderful to walk away thinking about something in a new way, to be encouraged to grow in your faith or be challenged by a new idea. Jesus has been doing this throughout chapter 8. He has been pushing his listeners to see him and God in a new way. However, the people have not been as receptive as he might have hoped.

The point Jesus is trying to make throughout this chapter is that the God the teachers of the law and other Jewish leaders are claiming to be children of, is in fact the God who is working in and through him, yet they are refusing to believe it. If they truly knew the Father then they would have known the Son, but they did not recognize him.

Jesus makes an enormous claim at the end of the chapter by declaring "Before Abraham, I AM!" With this statement, Jesus is claiming to be at least eternal, if not divine.

Read John 8v31-59, focusing on v48-59

{think}

Write down the ways people have been talking about who Jesus is and how they contrast with who Jesus says he is.

{reflect}

How are your expectations of Jesus challenged by the reality of his person?

{act}

How does Jesus' humanity and divinity change our perspective of him?

{pray}

Pray that we might truly know Christ and allow his presence to move us to action in our world.

**Journey through John
Lent 2014**

Sunday, March 23

{lectionary passages}

*Old Testament Reading
Psalm 95*

*New Testament Reading
Romans 5v1-11*

{sermon notes}

{think}

What spoke to you during the worship service today?

{reflect}

What was the call on your heart today?

{act}

What is something you are going to do or do differently because you encountered God today?

{pray}

Praises   Concerns

**Journey through John
Lent 2014**

Monday, March 24

There are amazing moments when we marvel at what we just saw or heard. When the quarterback throws a fifty yard pass into coverage and the receiver catches it for a touchdown, when the figure skater does her routine perfectly to the amazement of the judges and crowd, when the singer hits the high note flawlessly. What do we say to these amazing feats? "That was unbelievable!" When moments border on the miraculous we can't seem to wrap our minds around them.

Why do we have a hard time accepting the miraculous? We can see the wonder in the night sky, the blue mountains and their majesty, the roar of the ocean and the peace of a sleeping baby. But when it comes to seeing the divine supernaturally interacting in our world, we often can't believe our eyes. We think that we are being deceived by our senses. This seemed to be the same reaction Jesus received when he performed his miracles.

In the reading today, Jesus heals a man who has been blind from birth. The man has never been able to believe his eyes. After he gains his sight, the man's neighbors, people who have known him his entire life, who have probably given him food, cannot believe this man was healed. They cannot believe their eyes. They seem to have a hard time, just as we do, accepting the miraculous. They seem blind to the miraculous in the world.

{think}

What reasons do people give for not accepting miracles?

{reflect}

Who was/were the most blind person or people in this story and why?

{act}

How can we be more open to the miraculous and wonderful in our world?

{pray}

Pray that we might see the miracles, both big and small, that God is still doing today.

**Journey through John
Lent 2014**

Tuesday, March 25

We have heard a boss or a leader tell us, "It is my way or the highway." They will tell you how things are to be done and not ask for any input. I have worked for a few people like this and they were not my favorite bosses. Outside of the military, this might not be the most effective form of leadership.

In this passage, we have Jesus making two more I AM statements. (Appendix A, page 108) Thieves and robbers come into the pen over the fence but those who really want to be a part of the flock must come through the gate and will know the shepherd's voice. This seems like Jesus is saying, "I am the one in control and in charge, you better listen to me."

While these words might seem controlling, it is a different kind of power. Power in the world is used to bolster the one in control and subjugate others. But Jesus is using this power to protect and offer something more. As you read, reflect on the leadership Jesus is offering.

{think}

List the ways in which Jesus uses his authority.

{reflect}

Does Jesus the gate and the good shepherd comfort you? Why or why not?

{act}

How can we learn to hear the voice of our good shepherd better?

{pray}

Pray that we be the kind of flock that knows the good shepherd's voice and does what he says.

Wednesday, March 26

I have pictures on the wall of my office of my friends and me holding fish that we have caught. I like to believe it is to remind me of the good times that I have had fishing with my friends. But I think they actually might be there so that when I tell people how great a fisherman I am they will have to believe me because of the evidence, right?

People have been questioning what Jesus has been saying about himself. He seems to be claiming that he is God's son, therefore divine himself. The religious leaders have found this most irritating. But they are also finding it hard to deny because his works seem to be the works of God. Jesus states emphatically, "I am God's son."

Jesus has been declaring, and will continue to declare the union of the human and the divine as found in himself. It is this beautiful, mystical, wonderful, wild, strange thing that happened called the incarnation. God came not only to be with humanity but to be the Human One. Jesus declaring his divinity was considered blasphemy by the religious establishment. This is what has been upsetting them and what will eventually get him killed.

{think}

What evidence does Jesus give to show that he is the Son of God?

{reflect}

Why is it hard for so many people, both in the first century and today, to believe Jesus is human and divine in the same being?

{act}

How can we declare Jesus as human and divine in all our words and actions?

{pray}

Ask God to allow us to better understand and dwell in the mystery that is the incarnation.

**Journey through John
Lent 2014**

Thursday, March 27

When traveling, I do not like to stop until I get to my destination. If we need to get to the Soo, I want us to get in the car and drive directly there taking as little time as possible to stop for gas, food or just enjoying ourselves. If I am headed somewhere, I am focused on the destination and not the journey and when someone wants to stop for a few minutes to check out the sights or heaven forbid, use the rest room, I am more than annoyed.

In the passage today, Jesus is told his good friend, Lazarus, is sick. While Jesus seems to think it is urgent that they make their way to see his friend, he stays where he is for a couple more days. I couldn't imagine being one of Christ's disciples at this moment. I would be pacing by the door, making sure the bags were packed and being passive aggressive about leaving soon to get on with the rest of our trip.

Listen today as Jesus interacts with his disciples and his friends. We end this passage in the middle of Martha's statement. Allow her final words to remain with you as you reflect today.

{think}

In what ways does Jesus show confidence in what he is doing? Would you feel the same way if you were a disciple?

{reflect}

How would you have reacted to being one of the, disciples or Mary and Martha, as Jesus delayed visiting his sick friend?

{act}

How can you be honest about how you are feeling with God like Martha did?

{pray}

Be honest with God about times you have felt his delay in answering your request. Ask God to give you comfort when it seems like he is delaying without cause.

**Journey through John
Lent 2014**

There are movies that surprised me the first time I watched them. I did not expect Bruce Willis to be dead in The Sixth Sense, nor Darth Vader to be Luke Skywalker's dad in the Empire Strikes Back. These moments surprised me. They allowed me to see more about the story and illuminated events that had happened and would happen in the future.

Jesus has arrived at the home of his friends, Mary, Martha and the now-deceased Lazarus. The sisters had wanted Jesus to come and heal their brother. But Jesus was delayed and Lazarus had passed away. While the sisters show hope, they seem disappointed that Jesus had not arrived in time to heal their brother.

Listen as Jesus makes another I AM statement and John purposely records this as Jesus' final miracle. These two things are intimately intertwined. Who Jesus is and the power of resurrection are vital to our understanding of Jesus.

Don't forget to record the I AM statement in Appendix B (page 109) and the final miracle in Appendix A (page 108).

{think}

How does Jesus deal differently with the siblings, Martha, Mary and Lazarus?

{reflect}

Why does Jesus weep (v35) if he knows he is about to bring Lazarus back to life?

{act}

How can we talk about Jesus as resurrection and life in ways that will be meaningful to those outside the church?

{pray}

Ask God to show you where you may need him to bring new life and resurrection into you today.

**Journey through John
Lent 2014**

Saturday, March 29

It is the characters that make a great story: the funny ones, the tough guys, the warm hearted ladies, the gentle giants and the comedic goofs. How they interact with one another makes for interesting prose. Also, it is when these characters become involved in conflicts that our interests are piqued.

The Pharisees and the Sanhedrin are now plotting to kill Jesus. He is not traveling about publicly. In the final moments before Holy Week, the time period before Christ's death and resurrection, Jesus sits down for a quiet dinner with his friends, a time of respite before entering Jerusalem to the shouts of Hosannas.

Mary and Martha have been in a situation like this before (Luke 10). Martha is the one who is busy being the hostess. Mary is taking center stage in adoration of Jesus. And now Judas, the one who is going to betray Jesus, is enraged by the wastefulness of Mary. Read today's passage thinking about the people who are there at the dinner, who they are, why they are there and what they are doing.

Read John 11v45-12v19, focusing on 12v1-11

{think}

Identify the characters in the story and the role they would play in a dramatic version of this dinner.

{reflect}

Which of these characters are you most like and why?

{act}

How does Jesus defuse this conflict? How might we emulate that when conflicts arise around us?

{pray}

Thank Jesus for not shying away from conflict. Ask for guidance in an area of conflict or turmoil in your life.

**Journey through John
Lent 2014**

Sunday, March 30

{lectionary passages}

Old Testament Reading
Psalm 23

New Testament Reading
Ephesians 5:8-14

{sermon notes}

{think}

What spoke to you during the worship service today?

{reflect}

What was the call on your heart today?

{act}

What is something you are going to do or do differently because you encountered God today?

{pray}

Praises   Concerns

**Journey through John
Lent 2014**

Monday, March 31

It happens in too many action movies. The hero of the story and his forces are facing off against the villain and his forces. The audience knows that the movie is coming to its climax when the hero and villain face off. They come to the middle of the battle field. They meet in the darkened alley or the abandoned warehouse. They have their final battle and, of course, the hero comes out victorious.

In the passage today, Jesus predicts his own death, speaks about those who are unbelieving and finally talks about the final showdown. Notice that Jesus does not cast Herod, Caesar or the Jewish leaders as the villain. The villain, the one Jesus has come to defeat, is darkness. It is sin, evil, decay and darkness; this is what Christ will defeat through his death and resurrection.

At this time, Jesus is staring down into the darkness of the coming week. The next time he is in Jerusalem he will be a prisoner. He will be on his way to the cross. Jesus knows the darkness that is to come.

Read John 12v20-50 focusing on v44-50

{think}

How has Jesus shown who the Father is? What characteristics do you see?

{reflect}

How does Jesus' defeating darkness influence your thoughts on the work Jesus accomplished through his death and resurrection?

{act}

How can we show Christ in our lives so that we can say, "If you have seen me, you have seen the one who has sent me?"

{pray}

Pray that God might increase the aspects of your life and character that greatly reflect Christ's character and decrease the aspects that do not.

**Journey through John
Lent 2014**

Tuesday, April 1

One summer, my wife and I hiked Isle Royal for ten days with her parents and sister. This was a wonderful trip but there was one problem. Our feet, socks and shoes smelled horrible by the end. While we had sandals to put on when we got to the campsite for the night, during the day our feet were in hiking boots and not always fresh socks. And since our feet were our only means of transportation, they began to smell.

Can you imagine being in first century Palestine, where your primary mode of transportation was your feet? To make things worse, you wore sandals made of leather. Jesus and his disciples walked everywhere and more than likely at the end of the day their feet smelled and were dirty from all the dust.

The lowest job for the lowest servant was washing the feet of the guests who came to dinner. At this time, people would sit on pillows at a low table reclining against one another. Feet would be tucked up near their neighbor. Clean feet were important to them. So this servant would wash each person's feet as they entered. But somehow, as the disciples gathered to celebrate the Passover, no one had lowered themselves to wash feet. Except the one who has been claiming to be sent from God.

{think}

In what ways has Jesus demonstrated his teachings through his actions?

{reflect}

Why do you think this event was important for John to record for his readers?

{act}

What are tasks that you believe are beneath you and how could you emulate Christ in those areas?

{pray}

Pray to the God who humbled himself and became human that we might humble ourselves like our God.

Wednesday, April 2

I sat in our dorm room as I listened to my close friend pour out his heart. He had been dating a young lady at our college. He really liked her. But it had come to light that another one of his close friends had slept with her. He didn't know what to do. He didn't know whom to trust. He felt betrayed by both of them.

It is truly upsetting when someone close betrays your trust. You thought you could depend on them to be with you through the good times and the bad but instead you find yourself hurt by someone so close to you.

Jesus and his disciples are in the midst of their last supper together. Jesus knows that Judas is going to betray him. One of his closest friends is going to exchange his life for thirty pieces of silver. As a human, Jesus opened himself up to deep friendship and that also means hurt. Reflect on Christ's humanity as you read today's passage.

{think}

How has John pointed to this moment throughout the Gospel?

{reflect}

How is Jesus' model of openness to deep friendship and potential pain a model for us today?

{act}

Who is someone with whom you could deepen your relationship and what steps would allow for that depth?

{pray}

Pray that we all might know the joys of deep meaningful friendship and pray for those you know who have been hurt by a broken relationship.

**Journey through John
Lent 2014**

Thursday, April 3

It is sometimes the last words that we hear from a loved one that stay with us the most. It is the distant father finally saying, "I love you," days before his death. It is the praise from the grandmother in the last phone conversation before she passes quietly in the night. It is when people know that they are leaving that they often want to pass along the important messages in their lives.

Jesus is no different. He knows what the coming days are going to entail. He knows he is going to die and be away from his disciples. He wants to offer hope, reassurance, and comfort to his disciples. The passage we are reading today is the start of a very long discourse that Jesus offers his disciples on the eve of his crucifixion.

As you read, imagine you are a disciple during the days Jesus was in the tomb. Jesus gives a command to love but Peter is dealing with the fact that he was told he was going to deny the one he loved. Jesus tells them to trust in God and that they will also be going where he is going.

{think}

In what ways might these statements have been simultaneously comforting and disheartening to the disciples as they endured the pain of Christ's death and his days in the tomb?

{reflect}

How do you think you would have felt hearing these words without completely understanding Jesus was going to go to the cross?

{act}

How do we bring comfort to those who look to us for guidance in the same way Jesus did for his disciples?

{pray}

Pray that God will give us the strength that we will be able to love as Jesus loved and that we might witness to those who see that we are truly disciples of Jesus Christ.

**Journey through John
Lent 2014**

My father taught me how to fly fish and instilled within me a love for the art and sport of it. I love going out on a cool spring morning to fish on western Michigan's wonderful rivers or watch the evening hatch of the mayflies. While the very beginning of my fishing career was spent mostly at my father's side, in the last 15 years or so it has been by myself or with friends. My father will occasionally join me. But in the time since my father's tutelage, I have picked up a few more tricks and techniques. I have become a better fisherman because I had to learn things on my own, with the fundamentals coming from my father.

While I love fishing with my father, I loved the years that I didn't have him fishing with me as well. I couldn't just rely on him to know where the fish were, what they were biting on and how to cast. I had to figure these things out myself. I had to remember the lessons he had taught me and how to put them into practice. Some think it would have been better to have my expert fisherman of a dad with me every fishing excursion but this simply is not the case.

I have heard people say, "Wouldn't it be great if we had Jesus here with us right now? He could perform miracles and convince the world that he truly is the Son of God." Jesus did not think this was the case. As he was speaking to his disciples, he warned them that he had to go but he was not going to leave them alone. He was sending the advocate (the Holy Spirit) to be with them.

Don't forget to record the "I AM" statement in Appendix B (page 109).

Read John 14v5-31 focusing on v5-21

{think}

In what ways does Jesus say it is going to be better for him to leave than to stay?

{reflect}

How does it make you feel that Jesus trusts us so much that he leaves his mission to us with the help of the Holy Spirit?

{act}

How can we tap into the power of the Holy Spirit so that we can do the same things Jesus did?

{pray}

Pray that we might be worthy ambassadors of Christ to the world and that he might be glorified through what we do as a people.

**Journey through John
Lent 2014**

Saturday, April 5

As my family and I moved into a new house in the middle of July, we found the yard that had once been beautifully mani-cured was now overgrown. During the first couple of months of living there, I began to remove the weeds, prune some of the bushes and push back the advancing hostas. The wonder-ful bushes that were once prevalent were taken over by the weeds. They were not flourishing. With a little pruning and a little weeding, I was able to bring some of the former glory back to the yard.

Jesus starts off this section with another "I AM" statement (re-cord on page 109). This time he is saying the true vine. Tradi-tionally, the vine has been a picture of Israel. God brings the vine up out of Egypt and plants it in the Promised Land (Psalm 80). Jesus says that he is that vine. He is now saying he is the true Israel. Israel was supposed to be God's representative to the world but had failed to live up to that calling.

Now Jesus, as the true representative of God, is speaking to his disciples saying, that if you remain in me you might be pruned but you will have abundant life. However, if you go at it alone, you will wither and die. Jesus is in the business of providing abundant life but sometimes to get to the abun-dance, we must experience the pruning knife. Parts of us that are unhealthy need to be cut away to allow other buds to turn into flowers which turn into fruits of the Spirit.

{think}

What are the four different elements in Jesus' metaphor and what do they represent?

{reflect}

What areas in your life do you need God to prune so that you can have the abundant life Christ wants for us?

{act}

How can we allow for God's pruning in our lives?

{pray}

Pray that we all might accept God's pruning and support one another to grow in Christ.

**Journey through John
Lent 2014**

{lectionary passages}

*Old Testament Reading
Ezekial 37v1-14*

*New Testament Reading
Romans 8v6-11*

{sermon notes}

{think}

What spoke to you during the worship service today?

{reflect}

What was the call on your heart today?

{act}

What is something you are going to do or do differently because you encountered God today?

{pray}

Praises   Concerns

Journey through John
Lent 2014

Monday, April 7

We have it pretty well off as Christians in the United States. While there might be times that we perceive persecution, it does not compare to what other Christians around the world have experienced. Christians and people of other religions are being persecuted every day. A pastor in Iran is being held in prison with the daily threat of execution. Churches in China being raided at gun point. Christians in Africa are being killed for not supporting the local militia.

According to a report by Open Doors USA the top ten countries for Christian persecution are: North Korea, Somalia, Syria, Iraq, Afghanistan, Saudi Arabia, Maldives, Pakistan, Iran and Yemen. Because Christians are not the only religious group to be persecuted, we must long for the day when all persecution will end.

Jesus speaks to his disciples, telling them that because people have hated him, they too will be hated. His teachings are going to make his disciples at odds with those living in the darkness. The call to the disciples is to show God's glory and providence by continually proclaiming his name no matter the circumstances.

{think}

How have you seen these words of Jesus realized in our world?

{reflect}

How does it make you feel to know that some people are going to hate Christ and his followers?

{act}

How can we better support Christians around the world who are being persecuted?

{pray}

Pray that we might be the answer to our own prayer as we pray for those being persecuted around the world.

**Journey through John
Lent 2014**

Tuesday, April 8

I purchased my acoustic guitar as a freshman in college. Up to this point, I had only played bass guitar. I wanted to learn acoustic guitar so I could play songs by myself. I began to learn the acoustic guitar at this point, the chord fingerings and strumming patterns. I fumbled around at times. I got things wrong other times. I would play my acoustic guitar like a bass guitar. But what really makes the guitar sound great is when it is played properly. The improper playing of the guitar causes unwanted noises and usually hurts the ears of the listeners. It might even cause roommates to ask for a new assignment.

In the Psalms, the writers will often cry out to God to judge. We often think of this as condemning someone but in fact they are asking God to decide what is right. Righteousness is often thought of as a high standard that we cannot meet and it stands there taunting us. But righteousness is living as God has designed humanity to live. Let's say I took my guitar and began to paddle a canoe with it. It would propel me across the water but it would not be using the guitar for its intended purpose. It is an unrighteous use of the guitar. The righteous use of the guitar is playing chords and melodies; its intended purpose. But when we are called to righteousness, we are called to use our life in the way true to God's design. The Holy Spirit leads us in this. The Holy Spirit will show us the righteous ways to live our life.

{think}

In what ways is Jesus coming to judge?

{reflect}

How have you thought of the words righteousness and judgment before? How has that shaped your faith?

{act}

How can we judge what is right and live by those judgments in the Holy Spirit?

{pray}

Ask God to guide you through the Holy Spirit to live out the truth of being human.

**Journey through John
Lent 2014**

Wednesday, April 9

A friend of mine was working at a church as a youth pastor. We had been working on putting a retreat together and we spoke often during the months and weeks leading up to the event. But during this time, his church got a new automated answering service. When I would call the office line a machine would answer. It would offer me general information about the church and then the receptionist by pressing zero. Finally, she would transfer me to my friend's phone. It only took a few times calling before this game got old. My friend finally offered me his direct number. I believe, outside the office staff, his wife and I were the only ones to have that number.

There is something to having direct access to someone with whom you wish to speak. In this passage, Jesus tells his disciples that they are going to have direct access to God. While they will be experiencing great grief, the joy that will follow will be worth it. Christ's work on the cross is reconciling humanity's relationship with God. Humanity is no longer going to need an intermediary to get to God. Jesus is giving us God's direct line.

{think}

How do you think the disciples' grief mirrors a woman's pain and then joy in child birth?

{reflect}

Think about a time you might have lacked joy because you did not ask.

{act}

How can we be better at remembering we have direct access to God and using it to ask for those things we need?

{pray}

Pray directly to God. Thank him that we have direct access because of Jesus. Pour out your griefs to God and remember your joys.

**Journey through John
Lent 2014**

Thursday, April 10

One summer I was on a team of college students that travelled to different Christian youth camps throughout Michigan, Indiana and Pennsylvania to promote our college and help with the programming. At one camp, we quickly realized that nothing had really been planned. Study times were not planned, recreational games were not organized, and staffing was at a minimum. The first day went from bad to worse. The youth were bored. We were overworked trying to fill in the blanks. My team and I just wanted to leave. But late in the afternoon one of my team members said, "Well, if they didn't plan anything, let's just start planning and see if we can make the best of this week." With her encouragement we tried to make the best of the week and had a lot of fun along the way.

When things go bad, our first reaction is often to leave. We want to avoid the conflict and the turmoil. But this isn't always what God has in mind for us. Jesus has ended his lengthy discourse to his disciples and now enters a time of prayer. He wants them to know that he is going to be glorified even if it does not look like that through the dark days of Holy Week. He wants his disciples to know that they may feel like they are ready to just escape from the world, but his disciples are meant to be a force for good in the world, no matter how badly things are going around them.

Read John 17v1-19 focusing on v13-19

{think}

Where have you found yourself wanting to leave because of a conflict or awkward situation?

{reflect}

Why does Jesus pray for protection for his disciples rather than their removal from the situation?

{act}

How could you be a force for good in a conflict or awkward situation?

{pray}

Pray that we might not flee from a conflict or turmoil but rather look for ways to be a reconciling force of love.

**Journey through John
Lent 2014**

Friday, April 11

When I was in high school, a friend asked me if I wanted to be in his punk rock band. I had fooled around with the guitar and bass before but not with any real dedication. I decided I would give it a try and I went and got a bass guitar and amp. At our first practice, the drummer and I, with our new instruments, didn't really know what we were doing. Our guitarist, who had been playing for years, was great and really knew what he was doing. So we all kept practicing separately and together until finally there was that moment when we were all playing the same song, in tune with one another, on the same beat and there was unity. What had once sounded like random sounds of pained creatures now sounded like three musicians playing as one!

Unity can be a hard goal to achieve. We have seen the many ways the church has been divided and not played well together. Much like a band trying to find their sound, there is a time that we had to decide that we wanted to play together and make a harmonious sound. Jesus ends with a prayer for unity among those who are following him.

{think}

What does Jesus say will be the byproduct of his followers' unity?

{reflect}

How have we, as Christians, shown unity to the world and how have we show dis-unity?

{act}

What steps can we take to be more unified in our congregation, with local area churches and around the world?

{pray}

Read back over Jesus' prayer and pray for unity to be shown through our congregation.

**Journey through John
Lent 2014**

Saturday, April 12

I have worked many weeks of camps and of retreat weekends. Often I have had more than one responsibility during these weeks. I would direct the staff, play guitar in the band, help lead recreation time, preach at chapel and give devotionals at campfire. These are fun, exciting weeks. However, a few years ago I was asked to do one task, be the chapel speaker. I did not have to do anything else. I was allowed just to focus on the one duty I was asked to do. I felt these were some of my best chapel messages.

There is something important to knowing your purpose, the one task you have at hand. In the passage today Jesus is going to be arrested but listen as he encounters those who have come to arrest him. He knows what he needs to be doing. He knows he is headed to the cross. He will not allow Peter or anyone to distract him from his mission and the way the mission is going to end.

{think}

In what ways is Jesus resolute in his mission?

{reflect}

How do you think you would feel if you were one of Jesus' disciples watching him be arrested? How would you have reacted?

{act}

How can we be more resolute in our mission of sharing Christ's love, mercy, grace and compassion in the world?

{pray}

Ask God to show you his mission for you and ask for the resolution to stay focused on that task.

Journey through John
Lent 2014

Palm Sunday, April 13

{lectionary passages}

Old Testament Reading
Isaiah 50v4-9a

New Testament Reading
Matthew 21v1-11

{sermon notes}

{think}

What spoke to you during the worship service today?

{reflect}

What was the call on your heart today?

{act}

What is something you are going to do or do differently because you encountered God today?

{pray}

Praises   Concerns

**Journey through John
Lent 2014**

We had been friends for quite some time. He had helped me through a pretty difficult time in my own life, but I let him down. We were preparing to do a youth group lesson together. We were talking about trusting God. We wanted to show how we can trust God by having one of us fall backwards and the other one catch him. My friend had never done a trust fall before because he did not really want to trust anyone that much. But he agreed to do it this time. In my youthfulness, I thought it would make a great illustration if I let him fall and then we could talk about humans can let you down but God will not. I let him fall to the ground without even slowing his fall. He was hurt, physically and emotionally. When I realized what I had done, I was crushed. It took a fair amount of time for our relationship to be rebuilt.

Jesus has already predicted that Peter is going to deny him three times. But when it comes to the actual act, notice how John bookends Jesus before the High Priest with Peter's denial. As you read, put yourself in different peoples' shoes: the disciple who is with Jesus in the house of the High Priest, Peter who is denying Jesus and Jesus himself, who is being accused by the people he came to save. Let the impact of this story envelop you.

{think}

How does the slapping of Jesus' face mirror Peter's cutting off the ear of the servant? What does this say about the ways things are going to go through this night?

{reflect}

Who did you identify with most in the passage and why?

{act}

How can we be more like Jesus in this story?

{pray}

Ask God for the strength to stand for the truth in all situations.

**Journey through John
Lent 2014**

Tuesday, April 15

One of my favorite winter games in the school yard was king of the mountain. The school would create huge piles of snow on which we would then play. One child would head to the top and all the other children would try to dethrone the "king." It was a violent game that had real life implications. I cannot imagine they allow children to play this game anymore.

There are two ways that one becomes a king, either through inheritance or violence. The Jewish leaders are saying Jesus is King of the Jews which is making the Roman government nervous because they think there might be a revolt. What has been missed by everyone is that Jesus is bringing a different kind of kingdom. One that does not start with killing others but with laying down his own life. One that does not have geographic boundaries but transcends borders. One that is not ruled with a strong arm but with love. One that does not oppress and control people but rather lifts them up. Jesus has been declaring this since his ministry has began and now he is about to be crowned king of his kingdom.

{think}

How is Jesus reflecting the values of his kingdom through this interaction with Pilate?

{reflect}

Why are these values so difficult to live out in our lives?

{act}

How can we show Jesus as King in all the areas of our life?

{pray}

Pray the Lord's Prayer, taking time to meditate on the lines, "Your kingdom come, your will be done on earth as it is in heaven."

Journey through John
Lent 2014

My mind had been racing for days. My gut had been in knots. I was going to have to confront my superior about his misconduct. I thought about what I was going to say. I pondered the ramifications these actions might have. But finally I made the tough decision to walk into his office and begin the conversation. During the confrontation, my fears and nervousness did not dissipate. Rather, they grew. Over the next few days, I wondered if I had made the right decision, if anything was going to change, if I had eradicated my career.

It is those painful, difficult, tough decisions that can define us as people. In the passage today, Pilate, the Jews and Jesus are all faced with tough decisions. Pilate has to decide what he is going to do with this Jesus. The Jews are deciding who their king will be. Jesus is deciding whether or not he is going to follow this path laid before him. As you read, listen for the reason each party makes their tough decision.

{think}

What were some of Pilate's reasons for doing what he did?

{reflect}

Why would Pilate's decision to crucify Jesus as be difficult for Pilate as it was?

{act}

How can we be better at making the tough decisions and following through with actions?

{pray}

Pray that we might have the fortitude to follow through on the commitments that we have made.

Maundy Thursday, April 17
Seder Diner 5:30 p.m.
Snider Social Hall

When I was thirteen years old, I was hit by a Bronco truck while riding my bike. I flew onto the hood and then onto the side of the road. The driver of the vehicle and many other bystanders came to my aid. As a young boy, I had crashed my bicycle often and would "walk it off." As I lay there, people began to ask me all the questions that go along with having just witnessed an accident. I asked them if I could get up and "walk it off." They kept telling me to lay still. What I didn't know was that I had lacerations in my right thigh and ankle and a broken leg. When they kept refusing to let me up, I said, "Then call my mom. She will make me walk this off!" They asked for her phone number, which I supplied and she arrived on the scene shortly. She did not let me get up.

There is something comforting about having your mother around. She is usually the one we ask for when we are in any kind of pain, emotional or physical. Jesus, who is enduring a painful death, has his mother and close friends nearby, including the author of the gospel. But listen as Jesus interacts with her. All concern should be for the one dying on the cross but Christ has a different approach.

Read John 19v17-27 focusing on v25-27

{think}

What events do you think Mary might have witnessed throughout this day?

{reflect}

How would you feel as a mother as you witnessed not only the torturous death of your son but also people mocking him and gambling for his clothes?

{act}

How can we care for one another as Jesus cared for his mother?

{pray}

Pray that compassion and love might be shown when we are in the midst of both delight and pain.

**Journey through John
Lent 2014**

Good Friday, April 18
*Worship Service
6:30 p.m. Sanctuary*

The drunk driver came out of nowhere and struck the small car carrying a young woman. She was rushed to the hospital but it was too late. She had sustained severe brain injury. Her husband needed to make the most difficult decision of his life, to let his wife pass away and allow her organs to be transplanted or to leave her on perpetual life support. Through his tears he informed the doctor of his decision. A sorrowful day for one family was going to be a joyous one for many others. Even with the heavy pain of loss, the husband knew good could come of this tragic event.

It is interesting in the Christian tradition we call the day we remember the most horrific death of our Savoir, "good." Much like the beginning of Lent, Good Friday and Holy Saturday are solemn moments in our calendars. We are to reflect on Christ defeating sin, death and darkness through the sacrifice of his own life.

John records Jesus saying three things on the cross. The last two seem simple. The first reflects Christ's humanity. He is calls out for a basic need. In the latter, he is declares that his work, for now, is complete. He has accomplished his task and paid the bill. Today, as you read this passage, allow the final words of Jesus to sink in. Put yourself at the foot of the cross as Jesus speaks these words.

{think}

Why is it important for John to have an eyewitness when Jesus has his side pierced and water and blood flow out?

{reflect}

Why does John point to the fact that the Passover lambs are being sacrificed as Jesus is dying on the cross on the same day?

{act}

How can we live out the fact that Jesus has paid the debt and accomplished his task of defeating sin, death and darkness?

{pray}

Pray that we might live in the blessing that can come because of this awful day.

**Journey through John
Lent 2014**

Holy Saturday, April 19

The doctor delivers the difficult diagnosis to her patient. She then heads to the grocery store to buy cereal for her three children. Her day returns to the normal routine that it has been the previous days, months and years. For the patient and his family, it is anything but normal. Their lives have changed. The future is unclear. For the coming days and weeks, their lives will be consumed with this diagnosis. They are in the midst of the pain.

Today might be like any other Saturday. You might be reading the paper, preparing to take your children to one of their many events or having your grandchildren coming over, but it is normal. Can you put yourself in the place of the disciples, Jesus' mother or his other close friends? They have just witnessed the torture and death of their rabbi, leader and messiah and now he is in a tomb. What a sad, lonely, confusing day for the disciples! We know what Sunday brings, and it is hard to feel the sorrow they would have felt on this Saturday. Let us put ourselves in their mindset for a few moments.

In today's reading, a new character appears and an old one returns. Watch how these two interact with Jesus even after his death. The amount of myrrh and aloe that these two bring is one hundred times the amount that Mary had poured on Jesus just a few days before. If the amount Mary poured on Jesus was extravagant, this amount is reserved for royalty.

{think}

What do you think has changed to bring these two secret disciples out of hiding?

{reflect}

Why would Joseph and Nicodemus want to give a kingly burial to Jesus?

{act}

Where have you been a secret disciple of Jesus? What could you do to change that?

{pray}

Pray that God might give all of us courage to be his true, open disciples everywhere we are with everyone we meet.

Journey through John
Lent 2014

Resurrection Sunday, April 20

Taize Service
7 a.m. McCune Chapel

Family Easter Services
8:30 a.m. & 10:30 a.m. Sanctuary

{lectionary passages}

Old Testament Reading
Psalm 118v1-2

New Testament Reading
John 20v1-18

{sermon notes}

{think}

What spoke to you during the worship service today?

{reflect}

What was the call on your heart today?

{act}

What is something you are going to do or do differently because you encountered God today?

{pray}

Praises   Concerns

**Journey through John
Lent 2014**

Monday, April 21

Close friends of ours knew they were about to give birth to their sixth child. The normal excitement was diminished because we all knew that the baby would only live anywhere from a few moments to a few days. When the day arrived for the baby to come into, and soon depart from this world, we talked with our son because he was the same age as their first son. We talked about how we might not meet this child today, but we would meet him when Christ returns and all are resurrected. We grieved with our friends and our son seemed to understand.

It was just about Easter and I was talking to my son about the resurrection of Christ. You could see his little mind at work and he kept asking when it was going to be Easter and we helped him count it down. I couldn't really figure out why he was so excited about Easter. When I asked him, he said, "It is the day that our friend's baby will come back to life and my friend won't be sad anymore."

In this beautiful passage, John reminds us of the power of resurrection. There is something new that is taking place here. Mary confuses Jesus for a gardener, echoing back to the very beginning of John, the retelling of the creation poem. John is saying, through the resurrection of Jesus, that a new gardener has appeared, new creation is possible. Newness is happening all around us and will come in full one day. My son got the idea: there is a day coming when resurrection will take place and all things will be made new. It might not be this Easter but the great Easter is coming. We wait with anticipation.

Read John 20v1-18 focusing on 11-18

{think}

Who is the first person Jesus appeared to and what does that person do with the knowledge?

{reflect}

Why would Jesus not just return to the disciples with Mary?

{act}

How might we live in a way that declares that God created the world as something he deemed worthy of saving and redeeming?

{pray}

Ask God to show us places where we can partner in his redeeming and renewing work.

**Journey through John
Lent 2014**

Tuesday, April 22

My friend had tied the ugliest, most gaudy fly I had ever seen. He showed it to me the day before he was headed to the river. I told him there was no way any self-respecting fish would ever voluntarily take that fly. The next evening, he called to report that his new creation was catching all sorts of fish. I said to him, "I wouldn't believe it until I see it." The next week, we were able to get out to fish together. I saw fish traversing the width of the stream to have a chance to take his new fly. It took me personally seeing the fish take the fly, but my doubts went away. I will even use one of his flies, every once in a while.

Thomas was not with the other disciples when Jesus first appeared to them. He says he has to see the nail holes to believe that this is truly Jesus risen from the grave. Seeing is believing. There are many today that do not want to believe and John is calling them to see that the story of Jesus is more than just about an ethical code but a transformed life. Jesus, when encountered, will make us have the same reaction as Thomas.

{think}

What implications does Thomas' response have about who Jesus is?

{reflect}

Why does Jesus say that there are those who have not seen him but are going to believe and be blessed?

{act}

How can we help others believe that Jesus is the Messiah, the Son of God?

{pray}

Ask God for an opportunity to show someone Christ today through either your words or deeds.

**Journey through John
Lent 2014**

I have three good-sized book shelves in my office. They are filled with some of my books from undergraduate and graduate studies, as well as books I have obtained through 10 years of ministry and gifts from family and friends. I have them arranged in a bit of an order. Books on this theme are here and books by this author there. Books I really like to recommend to people are on a shelf at eye level and the books that have been given to me and I didn't really like are on shelves toward the bottom.

There are times that I will need a certain book for a study or sermon. I will stand in front of the shelves looking for that book and as I look I will see the titles of my collection and memories will flood my mind. I will remember the professor who made me read that book and the moments in class. The person who recommended this book to me and their guidance in ministry, the impact another book had on me. The discussion I had with a good friend in the late night over still another book. Finally, the books that were given to me of which I had read only a few chapters and couldn't get any further. Not all books full of memories but there are some that can bring back memories of moments, feelings and people.

John reminds his readers that the stories they have just read or heard are not the entirety of what Jesus did in his lifetime. Rather there are many other events, interactions and moments that could not be recorded. There were quiet dinners where Jesus probably joked with his disciples and other times where Jesus got up early to pray. These moments are not recorded in his gospel but they were moments of Jesus' life.

{think}

What stories from John's gospel account have stuck with you?

{reflect}

Have any of your views or thoughts about Jesus changed during this study?

{act}

How can we better show the library of Jesus' life in our church life?

{pray}

Ask God to continue to reveal who Jesus is to each of us as we continue to connect and grow in Christ.

Appendix A

{the seven signs}

1. _water into wine_

2. _____

3. _____

4. _____

5. _____

6. _____

7. _____

Appendix B

{the seven I AM statements}

1. _____

2. _____

3. _____

4. _____

5. _____

6. _____

7. _____

Made in the USA
Charleston, SC
25 February 2014